# "Karmayogi" And Other Micro-Stories

*An English Translation of "Laghu Kathaon Ka Pitara"
by Dr Yogendra Nath Shukla*

**Prof. Dr. Ashok Sachdeva**

**Ukiyoto Publishing**

All global publishing rights are held by

**Ukiyoto Publishing**

Published in 2023

Content Copyright © Prof. Dr. Ashok Sachdeva

**ISBN 9789360162863**

All rights reserved.
No part of this publication may be reproduced, transmitted, or stored in a retrieval system, in any form by any means, electronic, mechanical, photocopying, recording or otherwise, without the prior permission of the publisher.

The moral rights of the author have been asserted.

This is a work of fiction. Names, characters, businesses, places, events, locales, and incidents are either the products of the author's imagination or used in a fictitious manner. Any resemblance to actual persons, living or dead, or actual events is purely coincidental.

This book is sold subject to the condition that it shall not by way of trade or otherwise, be lent, resold, hired out or otherwise circulated, without the publisher's prior consent, in any form of binding or cover other than that in which it is published.

www.ukiyoto.com

This Book

Is

Dedicated To

Lord Shiva

Bhagwan Shankar!

The Creator, The Preserver And

The Destroyer

The Source And Fountain Power

Of All Arts

That Emanate From Him!

# Acknowledgements

**Acknowledgements** are due to:

- **Dr. YOGENDRA NATH SHUKLA** for giving me his precious permission to go ahead with the translation of one of his short story collections *"Laghu Kathaon Ka Pitara"* and the publication thereof entitled "Karmayogi and Other Micro-stories"

- **PROF. DR. VIKAS SHARMA**, Professor & Head, Dean of Faculty of Arts, Choudhary Charan Singh University, Meerut (UP) for his contributing his precious and very insightful and encouraging **FOREWORD** to this **Book**

- **PROF. DR. INDER DEO TIWARI**, Professor & Head, Registrar, Indira Kala Sangeet Vishwvidayalaya, Khairagarh (CG) for his elderly words of wisdom in the form of his pithy pointed **MESSAGE** and his words of blessings.

## DR. YOGENDRA NATH SHUKLA

Writer of

*Laghu Kathaon Ka Pitara*

ENGLISH TRANSLATION By:

## DR. ASHOK SACHDEVA

FOREWORD By:

## DR. PROF VIKAS SHARMA

Professor & Head

Dean of Faculty of Arts

Choudhary Charan Singh University

Meerut (UP)

MESSAGE BY:

## DR. INDER DEO TIWARI

Professor & Head

Registrar

Indira Kala Sangeet

Vishwvidayalaya,

Khairagarh (CG)

# FOREWORD

It incurs my deep appreciation for the exceptional translation skills of Dr. Ashok Sachdeva, who has translated 55 short stories in English from *'Laghu Kathaon Ka Pitara'* written originally in Hindi by Dr. Yogendra Nath Shukla.

Dr. Sachdeva's translation work truly deserves admiration, as it allows readers around the world to access and appreciate these remarkable stories. The collection of short stories translated provides captivating microcosms of Indian society. Despite their brevity, these stories manage to encapsulate the essence of various aspects of Indian life. Each story, spanning from a single page to two pages in length, serves as a window into the intricate tapestry of the Indian social fabric.

One of the notable qualities of these stories is their ability to be both illuminating and thought-provoking. Through skillful storytelling, Dr. Shukla offers insights into societal realities, shedding light on various issues and challenges faced by individuals in the Indian context. Dr. Sachdeva's translation effectively conveys the depth and intelligence of these narratives, enabling readers to engage with the profound messages they convey.

The style employed in these stories is epigrammatical, where ideas, thoughts, or sentiments are presented with accuracy and cohesiveness. Each story acts as a concise tablet containing pithy pointed, incisive sayings. This technique not only captivates the reader's attention but also provides a powerful means of raising awareness and triggering consciousness. These micro-stories act as conscience pricks or aches, prompting readers to reflect upon forgotten principles and ideals.

The stories incorporate incisive satire to portray the social, personal, and family lives of the characters. Through satire, Dr. Shukla skillfully highlights societal contradictions and challenges, offering a critical perspective on the prevailing conditions. Dr. Sachdeva's translation ensures that the sharpness and wit of the satire are preserved, allowing readers to appreciate the author's critique and social commentary.

The characters in these stories reveal their wounds, which can be physical, emotional, spiritual, or moral. They often find themselves as victims of the system or other social and psychological structures, grappling with the complexities of life. However, through their circumstances and struggles, they are compelled to reach realizations and rediscover forgotten principles and ideals. Dr. Sachdeva's translation effectively captures the depth of these characters, making their journeys and realizations relatable and impactful for readers.

These micro-stories also depict the harsh realities of life, including bitterness, misery, torture, poverty, and a lack of resources. Dr. Shukla's narratives portray these circumstances with vividness, evoking emotions and offering glimpses into the less fortunate aspects of human existence. Dr. Sachdeva's translation successfully conveys the raw emotions and stark realities depicted in these stories, allowing readers to empathize with the characters' experiences.

Dr. Sachdeva's translation also showcases his linguistic finesse and attention to detail. Translating literary works is a delicate art, requiring a deep understanding of both languages and the ability to capture the nuances and subtleties of the original work.The translation demonstrates his mastery of the English language and his skill in recreating the richness of Dr. Shukla's storytelling.

The impact of these stories lies in their ability to transcend cultural boundaries and touch the hearts of readers from diverse backgrounds. Dr. Sachdeva's translation bridges the gap between Hindi and English, allowing readers worldwide to engage with the profound themes and universal messages embedded within the stories. By making these stories accessible to a broader audience, Dr. Sachdeva contributes to the promotion of cultural exchange and understanding.

The translation process requires more than just linguistic proficiency—it demands a deep appreciation for the context and cultural nuances of the original work. Dr. Sachdeva's understanding of Indian society and his familiarity with the socio-cultural aspects reflected in Dr. Shukla's stories greatly enriches the translated versions. He ensures that the impact and intent of the original narratives are maintained, allowing readers to experience the same emotional journey as those who read the stories in their original Hindi form. This level of dedication and meticulousness in translation is worthy of admiration and appreciation.

Dr. Ashok Sachdeva's translation of Dr. Yogendra Nath Shukla's short stories is a testament to his exceptional skills as an English translator. Through his work, he brings to life the microcosms of Indian society depicted in the stories, allowing readers to explore the profound themes, incisive satire, and deep characterizations. His invaluable contribution in making these remarkable stories accessible to a wider audience, transcending language barriers and fostering a deeper appreciation for Indian literature. Some of the following features are worth mentioning during the process of translation:

Impeccable Language Proficiency: The translation work exhibits an exceptional command of both Hindi and English. His mastery of language allows him to capture the essence of Dr. Shukla's stories with precision and eloquence. The translated text flows seamlessly, retaining the original style and literary beauty, while ensuring readability for English-speaking audiences.

Sensitivity to Cultural Nuances: Effective translation involves more than just converting words from one language to another; it requires an understanding of the cultural nuances embedded in the original work. His translations reflect his deep appreciation for the cultural context and societal intricacies portrayed by Dr. Shukla. He adeptly conveys the cultural idiosyncrasies, customs, and values, enabling readers to fully immerse themselves in the stories.

Attention to Emotional Resonance: Dr. Shukla's stories often evoke deep emotions, ranging from joy and compassion to sorrow and introspection. Dr. Sachdeva's translation preserves the emotional resonance of the original text, allowing readers to experience the same emotional impact as the original audience. Through his careful selection of words and phrasing, he ensures that the readers connect with the characters and their experiences on a profound level.

Maintaining Narrative Flow: Translating short stories requires maintaining a cohesive narrative flow while condensing the essence of the original work. Dr. Sachdeva skillfully navigates this challenge, ensuring that the translated stories maintain their structural integrity and pacing. His ability to capture the essence of each story in a concise format showcases his storytelling acumen and expertise as a translator.

Commitment to Accessibility: Dr. Sachdeva's translation work plays a crucial role in promoting cultural exchange and accessibility to literature. By translating, he opens the doors for readers who may not be proficient in Hindi to engage with these captivating narratives. His dedication to making literature accessible to a wider audience reflects his belief in the power of storytelling to transcend linguistic barriers.

Collaboration with the Author: A successful translation often requires collaboration and communication with the original author. His collaboration with Dr. Shukla demonstrates his commitment to capturing the author's intent and vision accurately. Through their partnership, they have ensured that the translated stories retain the authenticity and creative essence envisioned by the author, further enhancing the readers' experience.

Dr. Ashok Sachdeva's translation of Dr. Yogendra Nath Shukla's short stories is truly commendable. Through his exceptional skills, he has brought these micro-stories to life in English, ensuring that their illuminating, thought-provoking, and intelligent qualities are preserved. His translation enables readers to delve into the depths of Indian society, appreciate the incisive satire, and experience the impact of the characters' realizations.

His translation skills encompass linguistic expertise and a profound understanding of cultural nuances and emotional depth. His translations of Dr. Shukla's short stories captivate readers with their impeccable language proficiency, cultural sensitivity, and ability to convey the intended emotional impact. Dr. Sachdeva bridges language barriers, fosters cultural appreciation, and enables a wider audience to engage with the literary brilliance of Dr. Shukla's stories.

# Professor Dr Vikas Sharma (English Novelist)

Dean Faculty of Arts
Professor and Head
Department of English
Chowdhary Charan Singh University
MEERUT (UP)

**A MESSAGE BY :**

## PROF. DR. I.D. TIWARI

Nowadays, when we hardly have time to read long novels and short stories that are actually not so short, micro-stories are in great demand. They are in tune with time and suit social media platforms.

We all know that storytelling is an integral part of our cultural heritage, and it has also been used as a tool to contain and evolve our socio-cultural heritage.

The micro-stories written by Professor Yogendra Nath Shukla and translated by Professor Dr. Ashok Sachdeva are captivating in nature. Professor Shukla wrote these micro-stories at a mature age. Professor Shukla revised this collection many times before getting it translated and published.

These micro-stories are micro in structure but consist of a beginning, a middle and an end. They are not didactic overtly and give the reader the freedom to imagine and deduce the necessary moral or lesson. Every story is like a miniature modern painting with many dimensions.

Professor Sachdeva has translated these stories into colloquial language that can be read and understood by any common reader.

One need not be a scholar to enjoy these sweet candy-like micro-stories.

These stories really hold the mirror up to society. I would love to discuss many of these micro-stories that kept on tantalising my mind for a long time.

"The Autobiography" is such a story. The protagonist of the story mistakes his social image, which he has constructed so meticulously with his ill-earned money and muscle power, with his real image mirrored in his consciousness and decides to write an autobiography. The human conscience in its purest form holds a mirror to every individual. You cannot lie to yourself. He is a representative character who lives in a society with many masks. He mistakes his mask for his face. He fails to reconcile with his consciousness and finally decides to do away with the idea of autobiography.

These micro stories, written in a simple and lucid style are open-ended and the entire collection can be read in one go. I congratulate Professor Y.N. Shukla and Professor Sachdeva on this beautiful literary endeavour.

Sunday, 3 April 2023 at 5:53 pm

**PROF. DR. INDER DEO TIWARI**
**Dean,** Faculty of Arts &**Registrar**
Indira Kala Sangit Vishwavidyalaya
(IKSV),Khairagarh, Chhattisgarh 491881
**Professor & Head**
Department of English

# PREFACE

The micro-stories of Dr. Yogendra Nath Shukla have been translated into Sanskrit, Sindhi, Urdu, Marathi, and Gujarati, and this is the seventh translation, which is in English. These Micro-Stories usually run from a half-page to two pages, are indeed micro-stories in the real sense, and offer microcosms of Indian society. The stories are highly revealing, thought-provoking, and insightful, and reflect social realism in the truest sense. An idea, a thought, or a feeling is conveyed in an epigrammatical style with precision and cohesion. These are small capsules containing the doses of the pithy, pointed sayings. These micros create awareness, bring about a realization, and also evoke, provoke, and trigger consciousness. These micros are, in fact, pricks or pangs of the conscience. The consciousness or the realisation is dawned upon at a social, psychological level or on a moral footing. This awareness is developed in the minds of the characters, or the protagonists, and also among the readers, and becomes a turning point in their very being. The characters are drawn from ordinary and real life, and they are throbbing, breathing human beings with their own idiosyncrasies, their own likes and dislikes, merits and demerits. The character traits are typical, and there are flat and round characters as well. The capsule anecdotes and episodes indeed offer touching irony and pungent satire on the social, personal, and family lives of the characters, who are usually caught up in some kind of turmoil in their lives or fall prey to the system. For some characters, the time is out of joint, and they are trying to settle scores with the situation at hand. There are ironic turns and twists, and it is usually at the end that some kind of truth dawns upon them. Some revelation is always at hand within the minds of the characters. The characters show their wounds, which may be physical, emotional, spiritual, or moral. The characters are sometimes victims of the system and other social or psychological constructs that hold them in their grip, and they strive to seek liberation either by surviving in the world or quitting it altogether. The micro-stories also bring attention to the moral and ethical issues that people usually and unwittingly lose sight of. But the situations in their lives evolve in such a way that they compel them and lead them to some kind of realisation of those forgotten values and morals. These micros show resentment, suffering, torture, agony, poverty, or lack of resources. They fall prey to the system, whether it is the police or politics, ministers or bureaucrats. All have been depicted with honesty and concern by the writer. These micro-stories usually begin at a critical juncture and lead the situation to a catastrophe until, in the final lines it takes a final turn and twist, either resulting in enlightenment, realisation or resolution, or even plunging into deep emotional pathos as in the story "Son".

The micro-stories are a great satire on the Indian system and convey certain ironic situations. Sometimes there is a grim kind of humour and pathos that prevail in these micro-stories. These stories make us aware of and generate consciousness about the loss of moral and ethical values in society and the sense of responsibility, the lack of which otherwise adversely affects the quality of life as a human being. These micros uphold the dignity of human beings and, at the same time smack of the human predicament and human existence.

These Micro-stories have fascinated me a lot for the message they convey, the values they imbibe, the emotions they evoke, the truth that they expose, the morals that they uphold, and the ethics and values that they nurture. This translation of mine is an honest endeavour with the goal of maintaining the author's original message which I want to spread to the readers of English.

The micro-stories of Dr. Yogendra Nath Shukla have been translated into Sanskrit Sindhi, Urdu, Marathi, and Gujarati and this would be the Seventh Translation which is now in English.

## Dr Ashok Sachdeva

Professor of English

(Former Chairperson,

Board of Studies in English, DAVV)

MJB Governement Girls PG College Indore

C 7 Shalimar Palms, Indore 452016 India

Mobile : 91-9926083522

Emails- *profashoksachdeva@gmail.com*

# Contents

| | |
|---|---|
| Prologue | 1 |
| Karmayogi | 3 |
| Big Vultures | 4 |
| Audacity | 5 |
| A Man | 6 |
| A Lesson | 7 |
| Shopolitics | 8 |
| Smart Son | 9 |
| His Father's Last Words | 10 |
| The Backward Wife | 11 |
| The Demons Who Gulp And Devour | 12 |
| The Great Hindi Lover | 13 |
| Farewell | 14 |
| Dog | 15 |
| Dreams Shattered | 16 |
| Theft And Fear | 17 |
| The Broken Soul | 18 |
| Treatment | 20 |
| Colours of Yesteryears | 21 |

| | |
|---|---:|
| **Foresightedness** | 22 |
| **Out Of Date** | 24 |
| **Agony** | 25 |
| **Infatuation** | 26 |
| **A Request** | 27 |
| **An Attachment** | 28 |
| **Humanity** | 29 |
| **Painting** | 30 |
| **A Meeting** | 31 |
| **Each One's Own Troubles** | 32 |
| **Harsh Reality** | 33 |
| **Burdonsome Parents** | 35 |
| **A Sense Of Responsibility** | 36 |
| **Helplessness** | 38 |
| **Lottery** | 40 |
| **The Big Man** | 41 |
| **Life In Moments** | 43 |
| **Family Vision** | 44 |
| **The Glow Of A Dying Human** | 46 |
| **A Rally** | 47 |
| **Beggary Prospects** | 48 |

| | |
|---|---|
| Screams | 50 |
| A Report | 52 |
| Apprehension | 53 |
| Politosnakes | 54 |
| Goal | 55 |
| Loyalty | 57 |
| Regret | 58 |
| Each One's Own Prayers | 59 |
| Changing Parameters | 60 |
| Each One's Own Dreams | 61 |
| Motherhood | 62 |
| Motherly Deal | 63 |
| His Brains | 65 |
| Mistake | 67 |
| A Half Army Soldier | 69 |
| About The Translator | 70 |
| About the Author | 72 |

# PROLOGUE

"Translation'is performing the important task of uniting the whole world in one thread. There is a foreign saying that translations are deceptive, and many similar misconceptions are prevalent about translationsn.

Most of the misconceptions arise because many times the translator does not have linguistic ability, or he does not have penetrating insight into literature, or he does not have creative talent. If these three elements are there in the translator, then undoubtedly a better translation will come before the readers. Just as the original writing can be substandard, so can the translation, depending on the translator. Actually, the task of translation is very difficult because the original author has complete freedom to express his thoughts, while the translator has to walk in a bounded way. He cannot add or alter, increase or decrease anything even if he wants, that is why some scholars consider the work of a translator to be more difficult than writing of the work itself. Today translation is working as a bridge between people of two different languages. It is teaching us the lesson of unity and integrity by promoting the spirit of "one world one family". There is a big difference between the re-telling of the Vedic era and the translations of today. The last century is considered to be an era of translation, the reason for this is that the heights achieved by translation in the century were not attained earlier. Again, the nature of narration has changed today. The exchange of literature that has taken place in the world has been possible only through this creative art of translation. Today, sitting at home, we are reading Shakespeare, Mopasa, and Maxim Gorky in Hindi, and in the same way, foreigners are reading Tulsidas, Premchandra, Rabindranath Tagore, Nirala etc. If there were no translations, could it be possible? To establish unity in the country, we have to take the recourse of translation.

When, Professor of English Dr. Ashok Sachdeva ji, expressed his desire to translate my short stories into English, I was delighted. In the past also, Sachdeva ji had translated some of my short stories into English and they were also published. He is a scholar. He is also a poet and critic. He has equal command of both English and Hindi languages. He understands the essence of literature, I am sure that he must have completely taken care of the original sentiment of the author. I will never be able to get out of their debt.

This is pertinent to make a special mention that all the images and Graphic Designs have been made by the Translator and the Editor Dr Ashok Sachdeva himself.

## DR. YOGENDRANATH SHUKLA

Former Professor (Hindi)

and Former Principal

Nirbhay Singh Patel Government Science

College, Indore (M.P.)

Res- 390, Sudama Nagar, A-Sector,

Annapurna Marg, Indore - 452009

Tel- 0731- 2483893. Mobile –

9977547030

E-mail-ynshukla4@gmail.com

# Karmayogi

## (Work is Worship)

Almost in tethers, in worn out condition, his unclean clothes were quite ripped and ragged, which matched his brown visage, and as soon as he boarded the compartment of the train carrying a small dirty bag and a flute his hand, he bumped into a young man.

"Have you no eyes…Are you blind? Can't you see while walking!"

"Brother! Excuse me, I am *Surdas* (a 16$^{th}$ century Indian blind musician and singer). Help me move forward, God will bless you."

Out of pity, the man gripped his hand and made him stand in the middle of the compartment.

He put the flute to his lips and began humming a tune.

'These rascals come to board the train and would stand anywhere! They are crooks; they run away with the goods as soon as they get a chance.'

These phrases that kept falling on his ears could not break his concentration, and he continued playing the flute engrossingly.

As soon as the sound of the flute stopped, people were delighted and started saying Bravo! 'Wah-Wah'. and some of them started giving him some money as a kind token of appreciation.

"Babu Sahib! I am *Surdas*, not a beggar! I make and sell flutes."

Everyone was amazed after listening to him. Two of his flutes were sold. He folded his hands to greet everyone.

He got off the train as soon as it stopped, and went inside the next compartment to teach the lesson of *'Karma'*.

# Big Vultures

As soon as a worker handed the list of names to Netaji (the local leader) of all those tribals sitting under a banyan tree, with their heads bowed down and their hands folded, expressions of tremendous delight flashed on his face...

The faces of those men and women were telling the story of their torn-down lives. The party workers had surrounded Netaji. Netaji addressed them and thus appealed:

"You should have clothes on your body, you should get bread both times, and the value of each and every drop of your sweat should be suitably paid for, this is my dream. To fulfil this dream of mine, this time also I have stood in the elections for your sake, I am your true servant... Eat and drink as much as you can to your heart's content..., I have made all the arrangements..., tomorrow is the election day...., and all of you can give me your blessings while comfortably sitting in your huts. I will get your votes!"

"Everyone now cheer up and clap your hands." The party worker instructed those tribals.

Suddenly the leaves of the banyan tree fluttered with a rustling sound ... "Sarr Sarr..."

Everyone could see, a vulture fleeing in terror from one of the ruins where cottages had been built, quite in utter panic and taking off a hasty flight, it flew up fast in the sky.

# Audacity

Mr. Mehra was the chief executive of the department. According to tradition, he hoisted the flag on the occasion of the 'National Festival'. He concluded his speech by saying in this way:

"...the nation is the first to be worshipped, it is paramount, we have to work with full devotion and honesty to take it to the pinnacle of progress."

Photographs were taken for publication in the newspaper and his views were also recorded. At the time of refreshment, Mr. Mehra was standing surrounded by the staff. Some complimented on his opinions and thoughts, while others praised his style of work.

In the corner of the corridor, two young officers were whispering:

"How come people speak so utter lies while standing beneath the national flag?... I am indeed amazed at their audacity!"

Hearing this, the other person replied:

"That's why his speech does not touch the hearts and it becomes just a piece of a notice put up in the office similar to the one that reads": "Don't make the walls dirty!"

# A Man

"Mr. Das! How does the new officer build up relationships around so quickly? He has full access to the senior officer's house and he can make entry and exit at his sweet whims. He has even impressed the MLA as well. I have heard that he addresses his wife as Didi!"

"Mr. Verma! I have worked with him. To prove his selfishness, he becomes someone's elder brother, someone's younger brother! He gains unrestricted access to people's homes by making their wives his sister."

"...But this is emotional blackmail!"

"You are telling the truth, but it has nothing to do with them. As soon as his ulterior motive is achieved, it turns out to be the end of the relationship."

Later, both of them got busy with their respective duties. They almost forgot what they had discussed.

At night Verma's son came to him holding a book in his hand:

"Papa! How did the man of the primitive ages look like?"

"Son! He was like an animal. He only thought of himself. Relationships didn't matter to him."

While telling this, for a moment the face of the new officer quickly surfaced in his mind.

# A Lesson

When his son got into college, he started getting heavily influenced by the current winds of the changing times. often, he would say such things to his father that he left his father perturbed.

Today, when both of them were leaving that store, the son proclaimed:

"Dad! If I were in your position, I would have made a fortune...!"

After listening to him, he understood that his son was saying all that stuff simply because he did not buy his son those expensive clothes.

He came to a halt after walking some short distance and pointed to the lock and key store on the footpath and explained to him:

"Son! I know the boy who is sitting in that lock and key store..., because of the sudden demise of his father, he had to drop out of school and run that store!... He might just as well try to earn wealth overnight by cracking the locks of any safe, but he is not doing such things. He is leading an honest life, and you, despite being so educated, think of doing acts of dishonesty?"

"Father! Please forgive me...!"

After listening to these words from his son, he breathed a sigh of relief.

# Shopolitics

When the riots did not stop even on the second day, the administrative and police officers got worried. They held a meeting and everyone agreed on a decision.

The roof of the collector's office was divided into two groups. All the officers were present there. A voice came from a group: "When both the castes have to live on this land, then why this riot?"

Similarly, the supporters of the opposing party also claimed: "The spirit of brotherhood has always existed in our country. It is the responsibility of we politicians to maintain it."

There, the leaders of both parties released a slew of such messages to the public. As soon as the 'peace meeting' was over, all the journalists started coming down the stairs. After coming down, a journalist's gaze was drawn to the terrace. There people of both parties were joining hands and greeting each other. Drawing his companion's attention to this, he wondered:

"If they had already embraced each other, the city would not have been in such a great misery."

The other freaked out and replied angrily:

"They don't care about the city… they have to set up and run their own shops in politics…. doing sheer shopolitics… as the elections are now drawing closer."

## Smart Son

As soon as Manohar entered the house, his father asked him:

"Why son! How was your speech? Well delivered or did you forget something...?"

"Father! The best speech on Gandhi Jayanti was mine. Some narrated the story of his childhood, then someone narrated the incidents of his simplicity.... I am the only one ... who told the incidents and episodes of the truth and honesty of Gandhiji. my teacher had also helped me mug up the content which I fully crammed and uttered".Manohar said keeping the packets of sweet 'laddus' on the table.

"Manohar, did you get two packets!"

"No, Dad!" Manohar said innocently, "I ran into the crowd again and fetched another."

The father opened the packet with a smile and while giving the 'laddus' to his wife rejoiced:

"Listen! Now our Manohar has become very smart indeed...!"

Manohar's face lit up on hearing his own praise.

# His Father's Last Words

The son could no longer hold back his frustration towards his father's constant tension-creating bickerings as he always took them to be.

"Dad, can't you just eat and sit quietly without causing some sort of trouble every day?" He vented. The son spoke to the father while fuming and fretting.

The previous night, the wife had taught him such a script that he exploded as soon as he came in front of his father. The father was shocked to hear his words:

"Son! If any member of the family does something wrong right there in front of my eyes, then I will have to interrupt... what is the point of tension in this? Ever since you deceitfully got my signature on the property documents, your attitude has drastically changed since then, at least, now, I beg you to leave me either at any old age home or send me to Haridwar for good! I'll live my own life somewhere anyway!"

"I would have left you a long time ago, but what would society say? Due to this fear, I keep mum and have remained silent until now."

"You don't care for your own father, but you do care so much for society, Son!....If people start having children like you, people will stop giving birth to children in the future."

He felt a sudden sharp pain in his chest. He slumped to the ground with his hands on his chest.

These became the last words of his life, that he could thus speak.

# The Backward Wife

Rachana's ever-present smile was missing when she visited her parents shortly after her marriage. Her parents felt she was fatigued since she had just returned from a long and exhausting journey. Her mother, on the other hand, could not be convinced.

"Son!" She exclaimed to her son, "I hope everything is going well with Archana."Isn't it?"

"Yes, Mother! In fact, I really liked the sister's in-law family and their home…They are well-educated and dignified… Everyone has conveyed greetings to you all."

"Son! I don't know why I feel that Rachana is feeling choked inside. I have never seen her so depressed before."

"Mother! I did ask Sister on the train, but she did not tell me anything".

"When the daughter showed signs of sadness on her countenance even the next day, her father became more concerned and panicked. He asked her:

"I have a feeling that you are hiding something from me…! Did you not like the family?"

"No, Father…all the people there are very good."

"What is the matter then?"

"Father! You have taught me through Hindi medium. You have inculcated in me Indian values, but all the people there are very modern and quite advanced. They even speak English at home. I do not know English. My brother-in-law and sister-in-law have often made fun of me… They all accuse me of being a slacker… a backward person. I do not even know how to behave in an elite society."

Having said this, she clung to her father and burst into sobs.

# The Demons Who Gulp And Devour

While serving the food to his students, the Head Teacher reacted:

"I cannot fulfil everything that a teacher ought to do for you even if I desperately desire to do so. I have to ride my bicycle five kilometres..., neither the bus nor the tempo comes here.... which is why no one is willing to come here all the way to teach you...! You know, when Sevaram goes on leave, I have to ring the bell myself. I have to help Sitaram make food as well...! In fact, I have tried my best to improve the quality of food, but in vain! The amount allocated for you by the government remains almost half, by the time it reaches me." The Schoolmaster started telling his woes.

Seeing the teacher getting so upset, a student began to console him:

"Master, please don't get upset... We understand your helplessness! My father says that these people are real demons.... they gulp and devour all the money given to us by the government."

"He has completed my incomplete statement," the teacher thought.

He patted him and moved on.

# The Great Hindi Lover

Prasad Babu's personal secretary had drafted and given him a piece of paper with the speech to be delivered for the program before he proceeded on vacation. He misplaced it and even after a thorough search, he could not find it. For this reason, he was pretty stressed and kept strolling in the room.

"Sir! It is time for the programme to begin now...!"

"All right... I will be there!" He responded to the driver and then again started looking for that piece of paper again.

His wife could very well understand the cause of his distress. She started explaining to him:

"Just as you often curse the opposition and know how to grind your own axe, in the same way, you start cursing English a lot today! ...the more you curse English, the greater the Hindi lover you will be considered."

The tension that was in Prasad Babu's face practically vanished as he felt relieved by her consoling words. He expressed his gratitude to his wife and stepped out of the house with greater ease to participate in and deliver his speech at the 'Hindi Day' programme.

# Farewell

Mr. Sharma was sitting on the stage, and beside him, his assistant officer, Girish was seated. Next to him, there was the chair of the senior officer, who had come from the divisional office and was invited to chair the farewell event which was organised on the occasion of the retirement of Mr. Sharma.

As soon as the Compere invited Mr. Sharma to address the gathering, Mr. Sharma stood up and walked to the microphone,

"Sir!" Mr. Girish whispered in the Chairperson's ear:

"Sharma had been sitting on the post coiled for two long years, and we were unable to make any money…"

"Now you will have your unfettered and unflinching rule. I will not transfer anyone for the next six months; you will now onwards remain in the sole charge. Girish! I have donated a heavy sum to medical college for my daughter and procured my son's admission to an engineering college. My expenses are also increasing. You know!"

"Sir! You can rest assured!… Our sad and bad times are now over," He began to assure the Officer.

Sharma's plight! He could speak only a few words on the mic. His larynx was clogged, and his throat felt choked. He slowly began to return to his chair, wiping his eyes with his handkerchief.

# Dog

"I have never expected even a single rupee from anyone in my entire career, and here is this officer demanding a bribe, and that too on money I have saved from my own hard-earned salary for the future."

He was cursing the officer sitting outside his cabin:

"You can go in, Sir has summoned you." Hearing the peon's voice, he went to the officer's chamber.

"Sir! It has been two months since I retired, but I haven't received the amount of 'Provident Fund' so far. My daughter's wedding is fixed for next month, and all of my work has taken a back seat, I cannot make any arrangements. Sir, I am not capable of offering you more than this!"

After completing his words, he put the envelope on the table.

"You can go now…. And come to my place in the evening to collect the check!"

The Officer instructed hurriedly keeping the envelope in his pocket.

Bansidhar arrived at the Officer's residence in the evening. He pushed open the main gate and stepped inside. The officer, sitting on the chair, was tossing a piece of bread in front of his foreign-breed dog, which earnestly pounced to grab the piece of bread being so flung at it.

"The Officer too had pounced upon me to grab the currency envelope in the same way…."

He thought bitterly as he stood still before the officer with his hands folded in obedience.

# Dreams Shattered

It was hardly a week since Amit was transferred to that school in the rural area. In the interval, all the teachers used to gather in the "staff room" and drink tea. Today, when all the teachers gathered, Amit expressed his resentment:

"I have been observing for many days that Antarsingh's cup is usually kept separate from all of us… I do not find it appropriate."

Hearing this, some teachers started arguing with him in disagreement. Seeing the matter getting serious, Antarsingh defended him:

"Amit! How long would you protect me? Why will you take my side? I am a teacher, but at the well in the village, I am given water from afar! You tell me …If I was not born in an upper caste family like you, is it my fault in this….? His voice became heavy.

Meanwhile, the servant brought the teapot and started serving tea in the cups on the table. Antarsingh got ready to pick up his own cup which was separately kept in the cupboard.

In a panic, he dropped the cup and it broke into pieces. There was an awkward silence in the room.

Seeing sarcastic smiles on most of the faces, Amit's face turned red with anger. He looked at the broken pieces of the cup lying scattered on the ground.

It seemed to him that the dreams of an independent India, so conceived by the freedom fighters, the makers of the Constitution, and the martyrs, to be free from any discrimination on the basis of caste, colour and creed, was now utterly shattered!

# Theft And Fear

There was an incidence of theft and burglary at the house of Sethji, the richest man in the vicinity. The entire family had gone to Ujjain to attend a wedding at the house of a relative. But as soon as they returned, they were shocked to discover that there was a theft in their house and a lot of hue and cry, a great uproar and a grumble in the house. The thief had taken away jewellery worth sixteen lakhs and about six-and-a-half lakh rupees.

As soon as 'Sethji' came to know that the elder son was going to the police station to file a complaint, he started scolding him:

"Look Damu! You don't understand when we are at our shops, our ladies will be harassed by the police visiting our homes at odd times. Whatever we have lost cannot be recovered, then, as a result, the income tax inspectors will too buzz around... they just want money...you know!"

"What a blunder I was about to commit!" The son thought and started returning inside the house.

'Oh My God!, I'm looted...!' harping on this string, Sethji started moaning as both father and son walked in, Sethji too followed his son behind!!!

# The Broken Soul

"The whole world has now indeed changed so much in all these past fourteen-fifteen years."

"The shops are also decorated in the city. The bus also started plying several times a day. Rickshaws have also started plying in the evening."

He was looking around very carefully with his blinking eyes. As the rickshaw was moving forward, he was returning to his past.

"Brother! Just stop the rickshaw!"

"... In this farm only, he used to meet Purnima... now she must have got married... almost he spent fourteen years and eight months he remained as a war prisoner in Pakistan... how long would she have waited !"

He gestured to the rickshaw puller to move ahead.

Everyone including his family members had assumed that Khushal Singh had become a martyr in the war. Today, as he saw Khushalsingh standing in his front all of a sudden, his younger brother's eyes widened with a pleasant surprise.

"Veer ji! Wahe Guru has sent you back to us…!" Both brothers started hugging each other. Tears of happiness had splashed out of their eyes.

"Dayal, where is Amma?"

"It has been seven years now since Amma passed away." With this, the brother started crying.

…Oops! Amma also left! He was shocked to hear this news! His hand baggage dropped down. He sat on the cot, leaning against the wall for support.

In no time, the news spread like wildfire in the whole town that Havildar Khushal Singh had returned! People kept coming to meet him throughout the day. After dinner, he lay on the cot. Many past incidents were still running through his mind….

During those fourteen years and eight months of captivity, he had to undergo so many tortures, and had suffered a hellish life. At times, he was deprived of food and even water ... he got only hurls of abuse and sound beatings; They had almost broken his body with physical torture. One leg had become completely useless.... At the age of forty, he had started looking very old...but he was broken there not only with his body...physically ..., he was too broken from within:

"Mother and Poornima... You may have both gone away from my home, my village, my life but not from my mind....".

Just as the thin water of the stream falling from the hill merges into the river, in the same way, the tears rolling down his eyes were getting soaked in his beard.

# Treatment

Because Prof. Mohan had connections with powerful politicians, previous Principals were hesitant to take action against him. The new Principal was very conscientious and strict in nature. He wanted the students to get the maximum benefit of Prof. Mohan's knowledge, so he tried a lot to bring him around, but he did not desist from his habits.

One day, a high official from the headquarters arrived unexpectedly to inspect the college. Some students were sitting and talking in a room. He enquired from them. He came to know that Prof. Mohan rarely comes to teach them. He inspected the college. Sitting in the Principal's cabin for quite some time, he gathered information and then returned.

The Principal put the Officer's written note which was meant for Prof. Mohan under the glass of his table. The officer had written to him giving a warning that the goal of a teacher's life is to enlighten the students and enrich their lives, and those who deviate from this goal are rather incomplete teachers.

Within a day or two, this news spread like wildfire among all the staff members.

After a month, the Principal was talking to the Officer over the telephone:

"Sir! Now Prof. Mohan is coming to the College regularly. ...And also carrying on well with his teaching work. I did exactly as you instructed me to ...I put your note under the glass of my table instead of entering it in his 'service book'... "Yes! I will tear that note now"

"Sir! Your treatment proved to be a complete success."

# Colours of Yesteryears

"How times have changed that even after living under one roof, an individual is quite an alien... almost living like a stranger. It is the festival of Holi today and all are almost locked up in their respective rooms!"

"Those were the times when there used to be happiness everywhere, gaiety and gusto in the house on the occasion of Holi.... we used to wait and feel the arrival of Holi for almost a month before, but today...."

Interrupting his wife, Mr. Bhushan expressed his grievance:

"Daughters-in-law act like showpieces in the drawing room, and sons follow them like slaves. How and when would they understand the significance of this great festival?"

There was silence in the room for a few moments, and then Bhushan's voice was heard:

"Listen! This all-convenient huge luxurious house seems very small to me as compared to my humble house of 'yesteryears', though it was a very poor house even quite bereft of all amenities."

"You are telling the truth...!" Ramadevi said wiping tears with her attire. Many past scenes and fond memories of the old Holi were emerging in their minds, were getting drenched now in the past tranquil recollections of both of them.

# Foresightedness

At the end of the symposium, when Vijay greeted Ramkishan who was sitting on the seat of the chairperson, handed him over his card and appreciated him:

"I have come to know after listening to your speech that you do nurture a deep feeling of patriotism in your heart. I admire your sentiment. Today, the country desperately needs young people like you. You are welcome to come to me whenever you have any problem...!"

Two days later, when Vijay reached his office, upon seeing him, Ramkishan signalled the workers to leave them alone and go to the outer room. Making Vijay sit beside him, he asked: "What do you do?"

"Sir, I have passed M.Com in the first division. I have been looking for a decent job for about a year..., if you give me a job, not only me, but my entire family will be grateful to you...! My father is a clerk in a government office. He has the responsibility of my sister's marriage on his old shoulders. I wish I could lighten that..."

"Vijay! Nowadays there is no future in any job, but the future lies in the man who holds the job...Even if you do not have any employment prospects, today the nation is in dire need of energetic young people like you...... If you want, I can help you procure for you a very high position in politics...!"

".... But sir, I don't even know the ABC of politics."

"Son! No Degree is required to become a politician. Politics need no formal education. You will learn everything if you just work with me for a few days. Yes, pay close attention to what I have to tell you. Today's politics is not the same as before, so even I have to keep pace with the times... You will have to maintain the secrecy of my work a secret."

"Sir! Rest assured."

"Vijay! Politics cannot be done on an empty stomach. Keep this handy..."

Ramkishan explained this while handing him a package of hundreds of rupees. Greeting him, Vijay, took his leave.

As soon as Vijay stepped outside, the workers rushed inside. Ramkishan began to speak to them, elaborating:

"I have included this boy in my group. He is quite knowledgeable. Elections are going to be held after a year... he will draft speeches for me. He will address my gatherings and meetings. If we have ten such boys, I can win the election easily sitting at home."

"Big Brother, I admire your foresightedness." A senior worker said very excitedly.Many heads nodded in accord as this statement was made.

## Out Of Date

"Mom, let me go in for engineering studies, and then wait and watch, I will change the condition of my house .... I will never ever do any job like my father!"

Mother's hands came to a sudden halt while cutting the vegetables, after listening to what Dinesh had just said. She suddenly started staring at her son.

"Mother! What I have experienced is that an honest man is put to the test while being ignored in the department and even the family of an honest man pays the cost of his honesty, just like my father has always been undergoing... Children of my father's colleagues have always taunted me for my ordinary lifestyle.... Mother! I will show them that I am no less than them in any way!"

"But my son! 'Honesty is the best policy'...one must always observe honesty, only then one's life can be considered successful!"

"Mother! I have read all these great things in the books, but nowadays the world is running contrary to this dictum...... These things are now out of date in today's practical world."

Having listened to his words, her finger struck against the sharp edge of the knife and she groaned with the deep pain!

# Agony

He was busy polishing the pair of shoes, the task at hand. He took a glance at the sneakers. Still shining them, he began stroking and brushing them again.

"Babaji! We have heard… Your son is a Deputy Collector…!"

"That is my agony, Babuji! It would have been better if I had no son!"

I got him educated sacrificing my own basic needs. And now that he has become successful he has disowned us. He thinks of himself as someone from the upper cast and doesn't meet anyone from our caste and community. What is the use of having a son if the son does not consider his father as his father?

He could now see that the pair of shoes were super shining but the shine of his face had now faded away.

…The glow and glitter of his face had drastically dimmed…!!!

# Infatuation

"Since the day you have come from America, why do I feel that you are not Mukul?"

"Your guess is correct. I am not Mukul, I am Jagtap…Suresh Jagtap… is my name."

"I didn't get you."

"You are not aware that Mukul married his own assistant scientist two months ago. That is why he avoided speaking with you on the phone."

"I just cannot make out what you are trying to say."

"You know, I have always loved you since my college days. When the relationship between you and Mukul started to get serious, I backed away, but as soon as Mukul got married, my desire, fire and passion to possess you got reenkindled. I was much better than Mukul in every respect. My only drawback was that I was ugly, so I got my plastic surgery done in America itself. I came back to India and disguised myself as Mukul to get your love back. I have put my whole career at stake for your sake."

Her eyes welled up with tears, after listening to him.

"I've been meeting you for the last three days, but my mind has been cursing me, so I decided to reveal the truth before we enter the wedlock. That is my pledge to you. I will keep you happy at all times. I asked you yesterday to arrange my meeting with your elder brother and his wife to discuss our marriage."

"I will talk to them this evening," she replied wiping her tears.

They left the restaurant and went to their respective homes.

The next morning, as he was reading the newspaper, his eyes widened with shock. A young girl, who was a scientist, had committed suicide! Her suicide note revealed that she did so because of her failure in love…!!

Tears now started dripping down from his eyes on to the newspaper!!!

# A Request

Small and large boxes were jumbled together and a clean bedsheet was placed on the top to cover them up. It was embellished with an image of Goddess Lakshmi and a few pooja materials and devotional paraphernalia.

There, two and five rupee coins were placed on an old silver plate and kept there... The room had a carpet spread on the floor. The whole family waited for the arrival of the father.

When the expressions of anxiety surfaced on the mother's face on looking at the clock, the son started explaining to her:

"Mother! How can he come home unless worship is performed and completed at the place where the father works as a salesman?"

"But Son! The auspicious time for performing pooja is running by...Hardly five minutes are left." Saying this, the mother began to glance at the door with keen eyes.

Everyone's faces lit up at the sound of the bicycle. The father entered the room, gasping for breath. Keeping the bag in the corner, he washed his hands and feet and immediately sat down to perform the pooja.

"Oh, Mother Lakshmi!" Bless my family with the capability of earning their daily bread with dignity... this is the least that I seek from you, Mother. If this does not happen, I would be quite disappointed, since I will have failed to fulfil even my most basic obligations."

His attention was drawn to his wife as he wiped his eyes.

She was still sitting with her eyes closed and her eyes were starting to get wet.

'Maybe she is busy praying and making the same request!'

His entire attention was now focused on his wife's face.

# An Attachment

While searching for a number in the telephone diary, his eyes stopped on that number. Anil Kumar Verma-2483838.

"What a nice man he was. His honesty and conscientiousness are even now talked about in the department. A lovely man has left the world".

He was on tour those days, so he could not attend his funeral, which he always regretted.

Now this name is not needed. He took out the pen from his pocket, but the pen did not move and remained motionless...

Despite the fact that he did not have a close friendship with Anil, ....of course, there was some bonding that both of them had always shared.

Sometimes he thought he would definitely enquire about his wife and children's well-being. He slipped the pen back into his pocket.

His eyes now shifted from that number and he started flipping through the diary in search of another number!

# Humanity

Bhattacharya moved to Indore six months ago after being transferred from Kolkata. His next-door neighbour Kanak happened to be a very quarrelsome kind of a man who had clashed with him many times over quite petty and trivial matters. They were not on speaking terms now and there was no communication whatsoever between the two families these days.

On the second day of Dussehra, Bhattacharya shared his thoughts to his wife:

"It is a tradition here that today everyone greets and hugs each other by offering sona leaves and seeking blessings from the elders. I am also going to meet the staff."

He plucked some golden leaves from the stems of Sona leaves, tucked them into his pocket, and left the house. As soon as he stepped outside, his attention drifted towards Kanak's father. He was sitting outside in a chair. Bhattacharya thought for a moment, then opened the gate, and went inside. He offered and put a sona leaf in the elderly man's hand and left after touching his feet.

Four days later, Bhattacharya was shocked to see Kanak's father standing at the door of his house

"Son! That day I could not give you the sona leaves... today I got a chance to come here. We are lucky to have found a neighbour like you... God bless you always." He expressed himself while offering gold leaves.

"Please come in Uncle and have a meal!" Bhattacharya welcomed greeting him.

"No, son! You know the nature of Kanak... if he comes to know that I had come here, then I will have to bear the brunt of his wrath and listen to his stinging words in vain."

Mr. Bhattacharya was standing with a dried gold leaf in his hand, and Kanak's father hurriedly went out... after blessing him.

# Painting

In the painting, placed on the table, a beautiful woman was feeding the child in her lap. Her body was exposed from different angles due to her torn clothes. As soon as Ankita's eyes fell on that painting, she asked in amazement:

"Mama! Who brought this painting?"

"Your father has brought this from Mumbai." Her mother replied.

"Such an image...."! This woman looks like a nasty beggar on the pavement, seeing whom we turn our faces away in disgust."

"My Dear Baby...! In modern elite society, such paintings are installed in the drawing rooms. Do you know its price …… one hundred thousand rupees in full?"

As soon as the father came home from the office in the evening, she put her arm around his neck and exclaimed:

"Oh, Father! You are so good… you know how to keep pace with the times!"

Papa smiled after hearing this praise! What a smart daughter she is! Seeing this, Mama's heart became happy!!

# A Meeting

"Mr. Verma, every year the department organizes so many programs…It is extremely expensive, yet there seems to be no significant benefit." The boss whined as he directed the waiter to clear up bottles and glasses and ordered lunch to be served.

"Sir! You are right. Everyone praises the mother tongue, but when it comes to preference, they favour English".

"As long as there is double-mindedness, nothing is going to happen…."

"Of course…!"

"How much money was spent on the programmes organised on the occasion of 'Hindi Pakhwada' last time?"

"Sir, approximately five hundred thousand…."

"Okay…. My car has been lying in the garage for the last fifteen days. You get the car right here for eighty thousand rupees. Spend the remaining amount on the events. Take care of all the formalities that must be completed properly."

When the waiter brought the bill after the meal, the Boss asked: "How much is the bill?"

"Sir, seven thousand rupees."

" Also, adjust this amount in the same."

The Boss concluded this meeting by instructing his subordinate.

# Each One's Own Troubles

Outside the hut, Babulal was wheezing and blowing his beedi.

When Chunnu's crying continued for a long time, he roared:

"What kind of mother are you... the child is crying and you cannot feed him milk?"

A fretful voice emerged from inside:

"You have money for alcohol, but no money to feed me... if you feed me something, only then I can feed the child!"

"The entire crop has been ruined due to heavy rains... What will the poor man do if he does not drink alcohol...?"

Spitting on the ground, he pushed forward towards the liquor shop... the booze store... quite determined!

# Harsh Reality

Examinations were taking place in that village school, which was now being inspected by a senior official who had just arrived from the city.

During the inspection, his steps came to a standstill and he peeped in through the window of the examination room. He was surprised to see that a teacher was helping the students write the answers to the questions asked in the examination. The Inspector started shouting at that teacher with anger.

The headmaster also rushed in there when he heard the voice. Immediately another teacher was assigned the duty in that room. That teacher was summoned to the headmaster's office. The officer's face flushed with rage, and he started scolding the teacher:

"What kind of teacher are you? you help your pupils cheat in the examination like this... How is it possible to set an example and create an ideal image of a teacher if you act like this? I will suspend you forthwith."

The teacher was hunched over, his head bent. He was standing with his head bowed down. As soon as the officer finished talking, he replied:

"Sir! We are only three teachers in this school. There are neither peons nor office workers. As soon as the session started, we were engaged to do the census duties, after which the work of making the ration cards was handed over to us. Then the duties for assembly and panchayat elections were imposed on us.

The Head Master will retire next month. He did as much as he could do as he was all alone. He had to teach the children. He had to make porridge for them and fed them.

For these reasons, the teaching work could not be completed properly. We were all afraid that if the result of the school deteriorates, you will take action against us. Thinking about this, we decided to help the children with the answers to one or two questions."

As the teacher continued giving explanations, The officer's visage gradually returned to normal.

# Burdonsome Parents

"When we left the house saying we would return in two hours; now it is night, but no one has taken any our heed so far. No one is bothered about us. You may not agree but the reality is that these people don't care a damn about us! He considers his own wife and children as his family. You call him and ask him to pick us up, if he really comes, I will accept that I am wrong in my approach."

Following her husband, Sunita called up her son...

" Hello, Hello, Son, it is me ... Your Mom .... Your father's elder brother had to go out on an errand unexpectedly at the last minute...…! If you send for the car, we will reach home tonight itself...!"

She listened to the son for a while, then said...... "It is all right, My Son! We will stay here tonight... and return home by auto rickshaw tomorrow early...!"

Seeing her face downcast, the husband enquired:

"Why what happened... What did he say?"

"You were right. He has just reached home from the office."

The son had answered :

"Why are you in a hurry to come? It is Uncle's house! why can't you stay there for a day or two...!"

"We usually feel worried and quite restless until our son and daughter-in-law return home safely from work.... But when we are out of our house, they feel that the burden is put off for a few days. This is the primary difference between parents and their son and daughter-in-law."

Her Husband's pain could be reflected in his words and Sunita's pain in her incessant flowing tears!

# A Sense Of Responsibility

While working, she used to look at the door time and again. As soon as she saw her husband, her sad face blossomed. She took the briefcase from his hand and remarked:

"oh...you have become so late today".

"I am only twenty minutes late." The husband responded looking at the watch.

"Ever since the tragedy of the bomb blast on the train, I have been feeling very worried about you. You also commute by train!" She answered while keeping her husband's briefcase in the cupboard.

"You remember, I had told you that one of the clerks in our office also lost his life in that mishap. Today, the Chief Minister has announced a relief of three hundred thousand rupees to the family of those killed in the bomb blast and also giving a job to a family member." The husband responded while changing clothes.

The wife brought tea. She placed the tray on the table and offered the cup in her husband's hand and expressed her views:

"The government has done a good job by helping the clerk's family... at least his family will be cared for and would be able to manage their expenses." Both started drinking tea.

"Listen! Today, while returning from the office, I was just wondering if I were on that train that day, my family would have got the money with which you would have got our daughter married off and the son would also have got a job......!"

"I am surprised that in all these speculations, you never thought of me, what would become of me without you….? You are worried about the whole family..., but not at all about me...You are less bothered about me.!"

The husband understood that she was hurt after listening to his words. He placed his hands on her hand and consoled her:

"Don't be angry… sometimes the side of responsibility becomes so heavy that one cannot think of anything other than it!"

Her moist eyes began to reflect the genuineness of the statement.

# Helplessness

You have also become like a common man, who never opposes tyranny. Pankaj abused you to persuade you and bring you around his wrong point. He vandalised the staff room and you have not complained about it yet."

Trying to cool down his anger, one of his associates persuaded him:

"Sir! You are a new-comer to this college, so you do not know the politics of this college! Our complaints are tossed in the trash here."

"I will not let this happen anymore. I am going to write a complaint letter, and all of you are going to sign it."

He began drafting a complaint after stating this. He obtained everyone's signature and submitted it to the Principal.

When he arrived at college the next day, he received a note from the Principal and went straight to the Principal's office.

"Come on, Suryavanshi..., how is your father's health these days?" Chandu, who was sitting directly in front of the Principal, asked him a question...

"All right, he is much better now, Big Brother...! If you had not got me transferred here, how would I have been able to get him treated in that small town? He got a new lease of life because of you." He said sitting on the chair.

"I came to know you have lodged a complaint against Pankaj... good that the Principal informed me in time... That complaint would have caused you unnecessary hassle if it had been filed at the police station... Pankaj is a promising supporter of my party... never make such a mistake in the future again."

After completing his talk, Chandu got up from the chair.

"Big Brother! Would you like to have a cup of tea before you go?" The Principal said with folded hands, but not paying any attention to his request, Chandu quickly left the room.

"Thank God …It is good that Big Brother was in a normal mood today, otherwise there would have been a ruckus. I admire your sheer boldness, the one who helped you so much, and above all the fact that you have the guts to lay your hands on the neck of someone who helped you out!" The Principal commented while tearing the complaint letter.

He was now sitting with his head bowed down as a culprit!

# Lottery

"Mummy! Today I went to Abhay's uncle's house; the entire house had been repaired and renovated, the furnishings had been organized, and a new car had also arrived...!"

After listening to the son's words, the wife looked at the husband's face and enquired:

"Why? Has Abhay Bhaiya won any lottery?"

"Take it as it is, he is my friend, I know his veins, know all his ins and outs. He spends money only in the hope of begetting money. Now he has to get his son married... and you know without all these things..., you cannot attract and invite good matrimonial alliances...!" Can you?"

The husband had now well presented the explanation of his friend's so-called 'lottery'!

# The Big Man

As soon as he came to know that Shyam had gone to the village, he turned the car towards the village.

"Mr. Verma! Of the two families, I like Shyam's family... You know that I have only one daughter, she should get married to a big man's family... she should live happily, this is our desire as parents. Ever since you mentioned Shyam in the telephone discussion, I had been thinking of coming here, but since I could not get leave, there was a slight delay."

"It doesn't matter.... Everything gets materialised by sheer coincidence, Anupam!, this is exactly the same type of family you were looking for. He has a great name in the field of politics and social service.... He has hundreds of acres of land.... I don't even remember how many properties he has in the whole city... He carries influence everywhere, all the facilities are there, your daughter will indeed live like a princess and will roll in happiness and prosperity." Verma advocted all this excitedly.

There was a huge courtyard surrounded by a wall. There was a big mansion in the middle. After parking the car outside the gate, both of them started going towards the mansion. They must have hardly walked some distance when they were startled to hear a sound coming from behind the bushes and started looking there:

... A man was tied to a tree and some people were beating him brutally!

"Bastard...! You eat Shyam brother's salt and you call him a demon ...!...You say he is a usurper of the land of the poor ...?"

"Don't hit me... I was drunk at that time, so it came out of my mouth, Shyam Brother is like a god...for God's sake leave me.... I will not say anything to anyone".

The man was crying and begging them for mercy and they were brutally beating him.

Noticing the expressions of stress surfacing on his face, Mr. Verma defended:

"Anupam! Without doing all this, one cannot become a big man today!"

"Verma! That boy from a middle-class family is much better than this one...."

So, what if the family is middle class...? He is an MBA, and he is only getting fifty thousand now, but the family is definitely cultured."

After having witnessed that scene, he changed his decision about any possibility of establishing any matrimonial alliance or relationship with that big man's house.

Both of them started now returning to the car.

# Life In Moments

Both the kids were looking desperately at the street:

"Mother! Just like yesterday, what if Bapu comes with an empty bag even today? Hearing this question again and again, the mother got annoyed and sent them out of the house.

Yesterday had passed somehow, but today it is getting difficult to spend every single moment. Since yesterday, not even a grain of food had gone into the mouths of the children.

'God, have mercy! Everything was going well, but suddenly the mill got shut down and within two months all the savings in the house were over. For the last two days, he would go to work in the morning and return in the evening with an empty bag.'

She was engrossed in such thoughts while placing a pot of water on the stove.

The children came back inside again. The girl went to her mother and proposed:

"Mother! If you allow me, I would bring you some bread from the neighbourhood. Deepu is also feeling dizzy."

"I had stored some rice. I am cooking it for you, your father must be coming soon." Mother assured her.

After completing her words, she began to apologise to God for this utter lie.

Just then a sound was heard at the door. Mother's happiness poured out of her eyes.

The boy started touching his father's bag and the daughter clung to him with joy.

Everyone's lifeless bodies became alive again in a moment.

# Family Vision

When the son did not find a job anywhere, the father helped him open a small general store with the amount he had received at the time of his retirement. He was not keeping well, so he wished that the son should get married soon. He also tried several matrimonial proposals, but the son did not like those very girls. Therefore, the father became suspicious of his intentions.

In the afternoon, when his son came home for lunch, the father inquired sternly in his heavy voice:

"Do you intend to remain a bachelor for the rest of your life or if you are already seeing someone…....? At the very least, tell me what kind of girl would you like to marry?"

He sat silently with downcast eyes. Mother served the plate in front of him.

When he left after lunch, his mother started explaining:

"Our Son is grown up now…. you should talk to him affectionately. He doesn't have any sister or someone to whom he can share what he feels and speak his mind…. I will ask him tonight, then I will tell you…. Don't know why you keep brooding over it for no reason!"

When Mother asked him late at night, he responded with hesitation:

"Mother! You know, the entire savings of the house have been invested in this store... I am trying my best to set up the store but in vain... The store remains closed when I come home to take lunch or go to the market for purchases... I wish I could find an educated and smart girl who would take care of the store when I am away."

He continued, "Mother! Expenses are escalating day by day and going to increase further, that is why I have thought of this. I dare not say all this to Dad. Maybe you can try to explain all this to him, maybe……

The next day when the son came home at lunch, the father thus endorsed:

"Son! Today, times are changing. Boys and girls are all considered equal. Your decision is correct. Son, my thinking was confined to the present, but your vision is for the future ..."

The Son started to look at the mother with a sense of gratitude.

Everyone's faces were lit up now.

# The Glow Of A Dying Human

My entire life has been a sheer waste! This pain caused him more agony than the physical wounds of the body.

He regained his consciousness after twenty-four hours. The entire family had gathered at the hospital. He was a prominent businessman in the city. He also owned property and had land in the village. He used to go to the village every Sunday. This time, while returning from the village, his car collided with a tree. The driver had died on the spot. Some people took pity on him and brought him to the hospital.

As soon as he regained consciousness, many scenes of his deception, acts of treachery and cheating committed to his acquaintances, business associates, and their family members began to surface on his mind's slate.

At night, he called the doctor and signalled the family members to leave the room.

"Doctor! I have come to know that tomorrow I will undergo surgery, in which there is very little hope of my survival... No one knows that Jasbir Singh, who looks quite hale and hearty at the outset, has been, in fact, a victim of mental disability throughout his life... Doctor! Now I want to die a death of a good human being, I want to make atonement by donating the organs of my body! I need your help...!"

His voice broke and tears welled up in his eyes. The doctor immediately completed all the formalities.

The other day while taking his body home, his bereaved family was surprised to see the remarkable change on his face.

The face that until yesterday had reflected feelings of deep pain and dissatisfaction, was glistening with the radiance, glow, glitter and sparkle of humanity.

# A Rally

Jagtap had taken his nephew Raghav, who had come from the village to roam around Delhi for sightseeing. There was a heavy traffic jam due to the rally on the road. They also stood on the pavement and started watching this rally pass by.

People running in the rally had placards in their hands, which read 'Hindi is the language of the people', 'Hindi is the language of the ministers-officer', and 'Hindi is the language of the grandfather and grandmothers.'

In the same sequence, the slogans were hurled "Hindi is the language of farmers, labourers, prime minister, chief minister, and courts."

"Uncle! If the language of all these is Hindi, then what is the need for this rally...?"

"Son! We have something in our minds and something else in our words…. We just want to display our love for the mother tongue…., we don't want to adopt it willingly in our practice."

On hearing his uncle's answer, Raghav felt as if the rally had become non-existent for him as it moved on.

## Beggary Prospects

"Now I have slept peacefully for the last three hours…. What a three-hour ordeal!... My heart was pounding in my chest. Have you ever thought how much sin we would incur? I tried to explain so much, but you did not agree... you got angry and pushed me to the ground... What if my leg had broken? She reacted looking at the blindfolded child lying on her lap."

Her inebriated husband's eyes blinked from the stupor fixated on her face as he heard her remarks:

"If you became lame-footed, you would earn four dollars more begging for alms…., you are talking about sin and virtue like educated people. Listen, moron, all of this is for the rich, not the poor. The slum in which we live is nothing short of an inferno... what heavens await us after death!"

While explaining, he took out a beedi from his pocket and started lighting it.

"You are very cruel…. The elder one ran away from the house scared of your beating. Even from him, you wanted him to go begging …. poor boy, don't know where he will be?"

She sobbed when she said this.

"He is the son of a beggar… must be begging somewhere else. Son of a swine will only sweep in seepage…"

Due to intoxication, he forgot to drop the fiery flower of the beedi and it fell on his hand. He shrugged his hand and freaked:

"It would have been better if we had worked as labourers, we would not have had to see such bad days, but you were always a work shirker…. You did not work nor allowed me to…. Look…look the blood is flowing out of his eyes…., you are not a human being, ….an animal…May you be destroyed."

The mother in her now had taken full possession of her. She had lost her temper on seeing the blood flowing.

Ignoring her words, he muttered:

"Khedaram was saying right. The cockroach has shown the effect. He had said that first, the child will suffer, when the cockroach dies then the child's suffering will stop and after some time his eyes will start bleeding."

Pausing for a moment, looking at his wife, he muttered:

"You bastard... I am making arrangements for our old age, and you are cursing me. Listen…. he is now eight months old. It is a matter of two more years, then he will start minting money…."

After completing his talk, he started lighting the beedi again.

But there engulfed more darkness in front of the mother's eyes than the eyes of the son.

## Screams

Rajeshwar was swinging on the verandah and his neighbour Govind was standing with his hand leaning against the boundary wall of his house.

"Our firecrackers are famous throughout our vicinity. This time also I have bought firecrackers worth fifteen thousand", Rajeshwar boasted.

" Brother! These days father's illness has rather worsened. The doctor says that his heart has become very weak. He needs rest and peace. He should take rest as much as possible. I request that you refrain from lighting noisy crackers this time. After listening to him, Rajeshwar stopped the swing with the force of his feet."

He thought for a while and then retaliated, "Govind! The festival comes once a year. We have to pamper the children as well! You can choose to close your windows and doors instead."

At around eleven o'clock at night, Rajeshwar returned with his sons after performing worship of Goddess Lakshmi at his shop, and the whole family started bursting firecrackers.

When the big bombs began to detonate and explode, Govind's wife became enraged and exclaimed:

"How insensitive they are! They care about their own pleasure, but don't care a fig about their neighbour at all! How restless Babuji is getting with the sound of firecrackers!"

Just then their son entered the room and informed them nervously:

"Papa! Uncle is making a very long string of loud firecrackers across the lane and. …. While laying it in front of the next house, he is approaching here."

Both his parents got worried after listening to the son.

"Stop him immediately" "Forbid them!" Govind's wife freaked out as deep panic reflected in her voice.

What if they don't listen to me and start fighting? No sooner were they wondering over this thought than the sounds of 'futfutfut…' started buzzing and horrifying them, even before they could think or do anything.

Govind's father started breathing heavily and fast due to the loud noises of crackers and his body became wet with sweat due to uneasiness. Suddenly, the agony in his chest began to throb…the pain started kicking in his chest and he started groaning!

Govind sat down and placed his hands held tightly held on his father's ears to cover them and his wife started rubbing her hands on his father's chest.

As soon as the sound of firecrackers stopped, the house began echoing with sounds of screams and wailings.

# A Report

The flag was hoisted in the school by Netaji, the leader. His speech was going on:

".... We have to make patriots like Bhagat Singh, Chandrashekhar Azad, and Gandhiji as our ideals, only then the nation will make progress."

As soon as the address was concluded, the courtyard echoed with applause... with the sound of cheers and heavy clappings. The Principal had assigned the task of recording 'Netaji's speech' to a teacher. The teacher showed the paper to his colleague and requested him:

"I have prepared a rough draft of the news to be published in the newspaper, can you go through it and review it."

The fellow teacher read the paper and remarked: "You must write only what the leader has said, otherwise he will get angry and the grant the school is receiving from the government will be soon withdrawn."

'Now we don't need ideals, but such ideal characters from whom the public can draw inspiration ... the nation has to be saved from those rascals with dual characters, only then the nation will be able to make all-round progress.'

These words written on the paper were now lying scattered on the ground in the form of pieces and he soon embarked upon preparing a new report.

# Apprehension

As soon as the sound of the car stopping in front of the house was heard, the father walked up towards the drawing room with the help of his walking stick.

"Son! I hope you had no trouble during the journey?"

"No, Dad!"

" Did the event go smooth?"

"Of course, Father!" Uncle was missing you terribly... I told him that you were not feeling well and could not make it!

"Son! Your aunt was a very nice person. You had to take the pain of travelling all the way to Nagpur. You must have been offended, though, but it was very important to join the thirteenth-day ceremony...although my brother's family is living in another far-off town, our blood is the same after all." Expressing all this, his eyes filled with tears.

At night, Yash came to his room.

"Look, Grandfather!" Papa has brought me these video games from Nagpur...!"

"It is really very good.... Let me see !" He appreciated as he was caressing his grandson's head.

"Grandfather! Mummy was saying that Auntie's 'saag-puri', the meal cost four hundred thousand rupees... Grandfather! Is 'saag-puris' so expensive?

Yash was looking for an answer to his question and his Grandfather stood aghast, motionless, quite apprehensive about his own fate in future!

## Politosnakes

He was walking on quite absorbed in his thoughts while nodding and responding 'yes-yes' to his friend.

"The clerk is a friend of mine, and he told me that you were chosen first by the selection committee. Your order was to be signed by the officer when he got a call from Banke Bihari recommending the other candidate who eventually managed to get that job...! Man, we do not have the recommendation of any political leader, which is why we have to struggle and go from pillar to post!"

His friend explained all this in order to give him a kind of solace.

They came to a halt as they noticed the crowd on the pavement. Some people were killing a snake with sticks and kicks. When the snake was almost half-dead, they hung it on the wall.

There was a poster on the wall that depicted that Banke Bihari was appealing to the public with folded hands to vote for him. Half of the snake's body was hanging on that poster and the other half was hanging on the other side of the wall.

As soon as he saw the poster, he uttered spontaneously:

"He is also no less than a snake. First, they would fold their hands in front of the public and then they would bite them. Someday he will be crushed in the same manner."

Seeing that poster, these sermons came impromptu out of his mouth.

# Goal

Today he was very happy. As soon as he came from the office, he enquired from his wife about Mohan's examination paper. When he came to know that his paper was good, he spoke his mind to his wife:

"You and I have suffered a lot… now we will get rid of all those troubles… today I am very happy… I feel that our goal has been achieved."

Both were talking, then Mohan came and touched his feet, he said, "Father! Now I have become an engineer!"

Blessing his son, he said, "Son! Are you planning to do a job or study further…What have you now thought of?"

"Dad! I have decided to go abroad."

"Why son… you are a topper, you will get a good job right here. You are our only son, if you go abroad, both of us will be left alone to fend for ourselves…"

"Dad! I don't want to work here; I have seen your life of deprivation and scarcity very closely. I don't want to lead a life like this anymore!" Mohan left the room after finishing his talk.

Mohan's mother reacted to her husband, "We have given him such a good upbringing, but today he is uttering such ramblings!"

When she started blaming Mohan, he consoled her:

"It is not his fault, it is the fault of the current environment, due to which youngsters have mistaken comforts and facilities as the goal of their life."

The joy of having achieved his goal slowly started fading away. He had somehow given solace to his wife and convinced her, but he was not able to convince himself anyhow.

# A Qualifying Degree

"Sharma ji ! Rakesh is often seen with Mr. Radheshyam these days... Is he also planning to get into politics?"

Sharma pulled a long face fell after listening to Mr. Saxena.

"Brother! Without offering some gifts or without any recommendations, it is difficult to get a job. Mr. Radheshyam is a leader, and with his kindness, my son may find employment. You tell me, if he had to do leadership (Netagiri or politics), I would not have asked him to do M. Com, after taking so much pain.

"You are right... we need a qualifying degree for positions ranging from peon to officer, but no degree is required to become a political leader!"

Mr. Saxena soon realised that unknowingly he had struck on Mr. Sharma's raw nerve which is why he had to mend his words.

# Loyalty

Everyone had left the workplace. He had to stay back till late today due to an overload of work. He was about to get up from his chair after finishing his files when his attention was drawn outside the window. Mr. Verma, a retired clerk, was approaching this way looking at each and every room. Until now, he had just heard from the staff that Mr. Verma would occasionally be seen here after the office closed. An office worker used to make fun of him by saying that even after his death, his soul would continue to hover in this office. After leaving the office, he instructed the poen to lock the room. Mr. Verma was very happy to see him.

"Sir! Everyone still remembers you… you are our ideal even today.

"Even I have not forgotten any of you guys and this office till now …My job started from this office and I even retired from here. Initially, there were only two rooms there… This new building was built in front of me… and with my own hands, I plowed the building. Those Bunyan and Ashoka trees that you can see were also planted by me."

Looking at them, Mr. Verma got lost somewhere. Perhaps some old memory that had been lying dormant had been jolted awake. He could observe the ups and downs of Mr. Verma's expressions on his face.

After some time, his attention was distracted and both of them started getting down the stairs:

"This office was my livelihood… It provided bread and butter for my entire family, so I find peace by coming here."

He said touching the last step of the stairs bowing his head in reference and walking towards the gate.

"If all the government servants were as loyal as Mr. Verma, then this department would not have been in such a miserable plight!"

He began to contemplate this, while starting the scooter.

# Regret

"How much does this pair of shoes cost?"

"Sir, eighteen hundred and ninety-nine rupees only!"

After hearing the price from the storekeeper, Dheeraj gently explained to his son:

"Puneet! Let me take you to another store... These pairs of shoes are too expensive!"

Both started coming out of that store.

".... Arvind's father and my father hold the same positions, but what a difference there is between the two, his father fulfils his every demand. All of his entire stuff is so good and wonder how much my father holds back while buying things?"

Not getting his favourite shoes, Puneet got agitated and began to freak out, and became quite upset at his father's utter miserliness.

"I dress you better than the clothes I wear... keep calm, I will get you some nice pair of shoes, Son! I cannot muster the courage to waste my hard-earned honest money like this...one should live by honest labour… you will understand when the difference between honesty and dishonest money when you grow up!"

After completing his words, his father put his hand on Puneet's head. Puneet could not look through his father's eyes. He was unable to raise his eyes even if he wanted to.

In his mind, the positions and places of his father and Arvind's father started shuffling and shifting now.

# Each One's Own Prayers

The wife was busy worshipping and her sick husband, lying on the bed, was watching her. She bathed the deities and wiped them off and placed them on a wooden swing. She applied sandalwood, turmeric, and 'kumkum' and offered flowers and the 'Bhog' of 'Misri', which was kept in a small silver bowl. After performing the 'Aarti', she started praying:

"Lord! You have given a good job to the elder son, give it to the younger one also, find him a job too so that he can live happily… his expenses are also increasing…"

Once her prayer was over, her husband sat up on the bed and retaliated:

"The elder son stayed with you until his condition was not good, as soon as his circumstances changed, he separated himself from the house… Now the younger son is all we have…, if he also becomes wealthy, the house will be bereft of children…!"

He folded his hands, bowed down his head and thus prayed to God:

"God! Don't listen to her prayers this time…!"

## Changing Parameters

A group of young individuals was debating the present circumstances and political scenario at one tea shop.

"Buddy! I was saddened to read the newspaper today. Now, it is high time we took a decision."

"You are telling the truth! Kanti Bhai hoisted the flag at fifteen places in his area, and our Netaji hardly at three places....! He insisted that the flag should be hoisted before eight o'clock. Because of these ideals, he is lagging behind. ...I don't think he stands any chance to succeed in politics! His idealism will destroy our future!" They continued to argue.

When they got up after ten minutes, their leader had changed!

# Each One's Own Dreams

Father! I cannot memorise very long answers in English, which is why I do not get good grades in the examination. I don't know how my friends can mug up and cram the answers …! I had also requested you earlier to get me enrolled in a Hindi medium school."

The son was standing there holding his 'report card' in his hand.

The expression on his father's face changed after listening to him. He had realised that this time too, the son could not get decent marks. He suppressed his anger and persuaded him:

"Son! I could not speak English fluently, which is why I ended up merely as a clerk in the company and could not progress further.... I want you to make your career to become a great officer, that is why I am taking pains to go to that extent and get you educated in an English medium school."

"But Father…!" Tears welled up in his son's eyes.

The father replied harshly, interrupting his words:

"Son! If you want to be a big man in your life, you will have to bear this pain….".

After listening to him, his son began to cry, but he was unwilling to make any compromises for 'his own dream'…!

# Motherhood

Ever since the days when Vinayak had joined the army, since then, Mother would step out of the house as soon as she would hear the postman's voice. The same incident happened today when the postman exclaimed:

'Mr. Sharma' and delivered the letter, and dropped it in the neighbour's letter box.

"Mother! No letter for you!" He answered as he proceeded forward.

"It has been two months since the death of my brother-in-law, but Mother still awaits receiving his letter." She conveyed to her husband.

While entering the house, the mother overheard her daughter-in-law say this.

"Son! I know Vinayak has gone away too far from this world, but I don't know why, whenever the postman comes, I forget this truth".

After completing her talk, the mother could not resist looking at the photograph of her son that was fixed and framed on the wall, with her eyes emotional and full of tears.

Both of them felt as if Mother was showering her bounteous blessing on late Vinayak to be 'Chiranjeevi', to be always Long-lived!

# Motherly Deal

Ever since Sudhir's family started living in the neighbourhood, the tension had mounted up and the parents became worried about Monu.

Sudhir was a government officer. He was affluent and there was no scarcity of money. He used to buy the newest and costliest things for his son Sanju. Sanju would always show those things to Monu, who would also demand similar kinds of stuff from his parents every day.

Yesterday, Sanju showed Monu his magnanimous beautiful pistol and flaunted:

"Do you have such a pistol...? My father got this for me on Diwali...!"

Seeing the pistol, Monu was tempted, too. As soon as he asked to see the pistol, Sanju ran towards his home teasing him by showing his thumb. He liked that pistol so much that even if he wanted to, he could not get it off his mind.

Today, when he went shopping with his parents, he got excited to see the pistol lying in the showcase of the store. When his father came to know the price of the Pistol, he found it too expensive and, he started convincing him:

"Son! Why don't you buy something else, …. instead of this, I will buy you colourful sparklers and beautiful firecrackers!"

"No" "No"…. "I will take the same pistol that Sanju has!"

He started reiterating this loudly while crying and whining. What would the people standing in the store think of him? Papa's face now turned red with anger. Mummy handled the situation. She whispered something into his ear and suddenly and surprisingly he became silent and gave up the thought of buying that pistol altogether.

At night, his father said to his mother:

"Since the day, he has made friends with Sanju, his demands have been increasing... He has been told so many times to make friends with children of his status, but he does not just listen...! By the way, what did you explain to him at the store that he finally gave up his stubbornness?"

"....Well, I advised him:

"Change your parents".

I proposed to him, "Sanju's parents are rich, they will buy you new things every day. Make them your parents....in exchange!"

"Well, Now I get it… that is why he didn't want you to leave even for a minute…..... look at him …how he is sleeping by, so clung to you!"

"Listen! Just now he was muttering in his sleep:

"Now I will never talk to Sanju.... I will never ever dare change my parents!"

..." Rest assured, I tried to bring him around after coming home and he has promised me that now he will never demand buying things."

His eyes were now fixed on Monu's face.

Oh! He is so naive.... so innocent! They started caressing his head with love.

# His Brains

Listen, I want a necklace exactly as the one Mrs. Sharma has got… Mr. Sharma is your colleague, if he can fulfil his wife's wish, why can you not…after all, I too have some prestige".

Before he left, this sarcastic remark from his wife was constantly pricking him. His mind was still brooding and his heart was still mulling over that. For the past few weeks, he had been listening to such reproaches from his wife. Even after contemplating a lot, it could not occur to his mind and he could not come up with any idea so far and think of any solution.…

Suddenly, the expression on his face changed. He asked the driver:

"On the way to Bhopal, how many of our government offices do we come across?"

"Sir, there would be four!"

"The meeting starts at twelve, if you drive fast, you can save an hour and a half. If we want, we can inspect two on the way and the other two on the way back home."

The driver nodded in agreement and accelerated the speed of the car.

During the inspection of the first office, he met the officer there and negotiated with him:

"Due to the breakdown of my car, I had to ask my friend to send for his car, so the fuel needs to be filled in, so talk to my driver waiting there".

Soon after completing the inspection, as he was having breakfast, the officer conveyed:

"Sir, ten thousand bucks have been given to the driver for petrol".

His car left from there. All the offices were inspected on the way much in the same way.

Due to the influence of his position, he got a car with full tank fuel, and will also get travelling allowances from the government...!

Moreover, inspecting so many offices in one visit will also make his senior officials delighted... and... and after that, he will not have to listen to the enduring sarcastic remarks from his wife!

The other day, when the car was returning to the headquarters and while reclining on the back seat, he was very glad at the performance of his duty with his great sense of wisdom and achievement that he really had had a good feast from his own brains!

# Mistake

Priya was a die-hard admirer of Indian culture, which is why Subodh always used to make fun of her by calling her orthodox.

This morning when Priya teased him with a remark:

"What a great love, the people of Russia had for their own language… we are the only ones who, considering our own language as inferior, consider it our great pride to speak in a foreign language."

Then Subodh could realise that Diya had made this sarcastic remark just to tease him.

Today, both of them were going to see and visit the house of Maxim Gorky, the great writer of Russia, in Moscow. They got off the bus in front of Gorky's residence. There was a huge crowd there, and a guide was narrating the story to the tourists:

"When the Russian Revolution became successful, the government chose this building on Kachalov Street in Moscow. Here, Gorky had spent the last five years of his life. The library in this house, his dining table, crockery and other belongings, etc. have been preserved with the utmost care to this day."

Since everything was said in Russian, Priya could only make out a little of the whole talk. Subodh was looking at the board displayed outside the house in which Gorky's brief biography was written along with his portrait.

"Priya…!" Subodh called out. When Priya came close to him, he briefed her:

"This is the house where Romain Rolland, Anton Chekhov, H.G. Wells, Stephen, etc. used to meet and have discussions with Maxim Gorky".

At the same time, they were surprised to hear a voice coming from somewhere, and both were shocked by someone commenting:

"How privileged and honoured the artists and writers are here ... and we Indians, on the contrary, are the ones who only perform the formalities just to remember them!"

This statement was uttered in Hindi by someone. When visiting Gorky's residence, a small group of four-five Indians were coming out of the main gate of Gorky's house.

Priya remained still there, but Subodh could not suppress his joy and went to meet them. When he returned after some time, he informed her joyfully:

"They were all Indian scientists. The government has sent them to this country for two months. They have invited us for dinner this evening! Words cannot express how happy we were to meet them".

"Come on, today you have understood the importance of mother tongue and Indianness…!"

"It was really my fault! Our language and culture are our identity."

Having said this, Subodh held Priya's hands and both started entering Gorky's residence.

# A Half Army Soldier

He is an incomplete half soldier, who perhaps could not get the opportunity to show the acts of courage and valour of bravery in his life. Whenever he remembered these lines, his heart would fill with sheer sadness.

Today, sitting in the garden with his colony friends, recollecting his army days, he thus moaned:

"I still can't adjust to life in Delhi. Here I recollect my army days at every step. There, the soldiers were always seen queueing up in discipline, but here I see that the civilians take great pride in breaking the queue... and violating the rules".

"Captain Sir! I wish if civilians had learnt this quality from the soldiers who had laid down their lives for the sake of the country, the character of the country would have changed."

After listening to the friend, suddenly he recollected the lines emerging in his mind that were written on the board of the parade ground.

Ops! He has been in the army for thirty years, paraded every day. Meanwhile, wars also took place, but alas! He never got an opportunity to showcase his valour.

Today once again, each and every word of those lines became a prick on his conscious and began to torture and inflict pain in his heart.

## About The Author-Translator

**DR ASHOK SACHDEVA**

• Professor of English at Indore and is the Translator and Editor of this book.

• He has been awarded 'Best Professor of the Year 2023 Gyan Bhushan Award'

• He had been Head of the Department & also Chairman of, the Board of Studies in English, Devi Ahilya University, Indore. (2006-2009) and Member, Central Board of Studies of English Bhopal (2008-2020).

• He was Principal Investigator in UGC Major Research Project 2011-14. He has been Research Supervisor & External Examiner of Ph.D and Visiting Professor at Indian Universities.

• He has Chaired sessions at International Conferences at the University of Manchester UK (Aug 2013), University of Toronto (Aug 2000), University of London, 2005, USA, University of Cape Town.

Plenary and Keynote Speaker at International Conferences in India. Resource Person at Refresher Courses for College Teachers in Indian Universities. He has lectured as Visiting Faculty at London, England.

- Many research papers and articles and Five edited Books, have been published by Hindi Granth Academy and two Books on Poetry Translation.

- Three Books Translated and Edited on Poetry *In the Web of Times* &*Fragrant Feelings,* and *Micro-Short Stories of Dr Yogendra Nath Shukla*

- Prepared e-content and audio-video lectures for the Dept of Higher Education, Govt. of Madhya Pradesh.

- He has been a Member of the Research Advisory Committee, Board Member & Board of Studies Member of DAVV.

- Served as Superintendent of UPSC, PSC Examinations, Observer in PSC &PEB Examinations. Screening Committee Subject Expert in Selection of Lecturers and Professors of Colleges. Member of College Inspection Committees. Convener of Legal Cell of Govt. Higher Education.

## About the Author

**DR. YOGENDRA NATH SHUKLA**

### EDUCATION:

M.A. (Gold Medalist), PhD (Anantasevi of Hindi Anant Gopal Shevde novels, the first Dissertation treatise on literature)

LITERARY ACTIVITIES: Creative Writing:

Published *Laghu Kathaon ka Khajana'* (2022) 'Laghu Kathaon ka Pitara' 2008) from Kitabh Ghar, Delhi. Published *'Shapath- Yatra'* (Short Story Collection-2000),

Stories, research articles. poems, memoirs. Published Children's literature, Satire and about 670 Short Stories in Hindi (Laghu Kathaen).

Awarded by Akhil Bhartiya 'Pragatisheel Laghu Katha Manch' and Best Short Story Book of 2008.

TRANSLATED WORKS-

'*Shapath-Yatra'*(100 Short Stories translated into Marathi) *Laghuttam Kathancha Guldasta*' (112 Short Stories translated into Marathi) *Kathanjali* (55 Short Stories with original short story translated into Sanskrit)/ Published 55 Short stories translated into Sanskrit in the magazine 'Arvachin Sanskritam' (Delhi).

The first short story collection was translated into Sanskrit. *'Badalte Piamane'* (117 Short Stories translated into Urdu) being read in Pakistan.

'Satrangi Short Stories' (72 Short Stories translated into Sindhi) and 116 stories *Badalate Nayak* in Punjabi.

*Diyan Mini Kahaniyan* (90 Short Stories translated into Punjabi). Micro-stories of Dr.YogendranathShukla (55 short stories translated into English). Many short stories translated into Nepali, Gujarati, Kannad, Oriya, Nimadi etc.

EDITING: 'Dainik Bhaskar', 'International Manas Sangam' (annual issue), 'Research-2000' (Research- Magazine), 'Vagdhara' (Short Story especially Issue), Editing of the compilation 'Samprabh'. Editing of the poetry collection 'Samay Ka Saathi', 'Haridra' (research journal), Editing of the research journal (2018) of 'Kafla International Writers'.

Ex Member: M.P. Hindi Granth Academy. Senate member of Indore University.

## HONORS & AWARDS:

Awarded by many literary institutions of the country for literary service and 'Dr. Parmeshwar Goyal' at the 21st All India Progressive Short Story Conference Awarded with 'Short Story Shikhar Samman'.

Current Position:
Former Professor, (Hindi) and Former Principal
Nirbhay Singh Patel Government Science
College, Indore, M.P.
Contact: 390, Sudama Nagar, A-Sector, Annapurna Marg, Indore – 452009
Mobile–09977547030
E-mail-ynshukla4@gmail.com

## PUBLICATIONS BY PROF DR. ASHOK SACHDEVA

- *MICRO-SHORT STORIES OF DR YOGENDRANATH SHUKLA-* A Translation in English, published at, Amazon. April 2022.
- *FRAGRANT FEELINGS: Poems of Dr Padma Singh-* A Translation in English, published at Amazon, March 2022
- Editor In *The Web of Time -Poetic World Of Rajendra Mishra* Edited By Dr Ashok Sachdeva
- *An Anthology of English Literature* for Unified Syllabus In Madhya Pradesh. Edited By Dr Ashok Sachdeva
- *An Anthology of English Literature-* Co-editor in Text Book of English Literature for Unified syllabus in Madhya Pradesh published by Hindi Granth Academy, Department of Higher Education, Government of Madhya Pradesh Bhopal, MP
- *Text Book of English Language* -Co-editor for Unified Syllabus In Madhya Pradesh Edited by Dr Ashok Sachdeva
- *Text Book of English Language for B. A. Text Book of English Language* - Co-editor for Unified syllabus in MP for BA Partil published by Hindi Granth Academy, Department of Higher Education, Government of MP Bhopal
- *Text Book of English Communicative English* 2021-22- Co-editor Text Book of English Communicative for Unified Syllabus In Madhya Pradesh
- *Text Book of English Literature 2022-23* -Co-editor Text Book of English Literature for Unified Syllabus In Madhya Pradesh.

## CH. CHARAN SINGH UNIVERSITY, MEERUT
### DEPARTMENT OF ENGLISH

Dr. VIKAS SHARMA
D.Lit
Professor & Head

General Secretary
The Association for
English Studies of India
(AESI)

Ref No............................                                   Dated 05/07/2023

# Foreword

It incurs my deep appreciation for the exceptional translation skills of Dr. Ashok Sachdeva, who has translated 55 short stories in English from *Laghu Kathaon Ka Pitara* written originally in Hindi by Dr. Yogendra Nath Shukla.

Dr. Sachdeva's translation work truly deserves admiration, as it allows readers around the world to access and appreciate these remarkable stories. The collection of short stories translated provides captivating microcosms of Indian society. Despite their brevity, these stories manage to encapsulate the essence of various aspects of Indian life. Each story, spanning from a single page to two pages in length, serves as a window into the intricate tapestry of the Indian social fabric.

One of the notable qualities of these stories is their ability to be both illuminating and thought-provoking. Through skilful storytelling, Dr. Shukla offers insights into societal realities, shedding light on various issues and challenges faced by individuals in the Indian context. Dr. Sachdeva's translation effectively conveys the depth and intelligence of these narratives, enabling readers to engage with the profound messages they convey.

The style employed in these stories is epigrammatical, where ideas, thoughts, or sentiments are presented with accuracy and cohesiveness. Each story acts as a concise tablet containing pithy, pointed, incisive sayings. This technique not only captivates the reader's attention but also provides a powerful means of raising awareness and triggering consciousness. These micro-stories act as conscience pricks or aches, prompting readers to reflect upon forgotten principles and ideals.

RESIDENCE : F-43, Shastri Nagar, Meerut - 250 004 (U.P.)
Mob. : 9410454723 • E-mail : drvikas.27nov@gmail.com, vikassharmaccsu@gmail.com

## CH. CHARAN SINGH UNIVERSITY, MEERUT
### DEPARTMENT OF ENGLISH

**Dr. VIKAS SHARMA**
D.Lit
Professor & Head

**General Secretary**
The Association for
English Studies of India
(AESI)

Ref No........................                                                Dated........................

The stories incorporate incisive satire to portray the social, personal, and family lives of the characters. Through satire, Dr. Shukla skillfully highlights societal contradictions and challenges, offering a critical perspective on the prevailing conditions. Dr. Sachdeva's translation ensures that the sharpness and wit of the satire are preserved, allowing readers to appreciate the author's critique and social commentary.

The characters in these stories reveal their wounds, which can be physical, emotional, spiritual, or moral. They often find themselves as victims of the system or other social and psychological structures, grappling with the complexities of life. However, through their circumstances and struggles, they are compelled to reach realizations and rediscover forgotten principles and ideals. Dr. Sachdeva's translation effectively captures the depth of these characters, making their journeys and realizations relatable and impactful for readers.

These micro-stories also depict the harsh realities of life, including bitterness, misery, torture, poverty, and a lack of resources. Dr. Shukla's narratives portray these circumstances with vividness, evoking emotions and offering glimpses into the less fortunate aspects of human existence. Dr. Sachdeva's translation successfully conveys the raw emotions and stark realities depicted in these stories, allowing readers to empathize with the characters' experiences.

Dr. Sachdeva's translation also showcases his linguistic finesse and attention to detail. Translating literary works is a delicate art, requiring a deep understanding of both languages and the ability to capture the nuances and subtleties of the original work. The translation demonstrates his mastery of the English language and his skill in recreating the richness of Dr. Shukla's storytelling.

The impact of these stories lies in their ability to transcend cultural boundaries and touch the hearts of readers from diverse backgrounds. Dr. Sachdeva's translation bridges the gap between Hindi and English, allowing readers worldwide to engage with the profound

---

**RESIDENCE :** F-43, Shastri Nagar, Meerut - 250 004 (U.P.)
**Mob. :** 9410454723 ▪ **E-mail :** drvikas.27nov@gmail.com, vikassharmaccsu@gmail.com

## Prof. Dr. Ashok Sachdeva

## CH. CHARAN SINGH UNIVERSITY, MEERUT
### DEPARTMENT OF ENGLISH

Dr. VIKAS SHARMA
D.Lit
Professor & Head

General Secretary
The Association for
English Studies of India
(AESI)

Ref No.............................                                                                Dated................................

themes and universal messages embedded within the stories. By making these stories accessible to a broader audience, Dr. Sachdeva contributes to the promotion of cultural exchange and understanding.

The translation process requires more than just linguistic proficiency—it demands a deep appreciation for the context and cultural nuances of the original work. Dr. Sachdeva's understanding of Indian society and his familiarity with the socio-cultural aspects reflected in Dr. Shukla's stories greatly enriches the translated versions. He ensures that the impact and intent of the original narratives are maintained, allowing readers to experience the same emotional journey as those who read the stories in their original Hindi form. This level of dedication and meticulousness in translation is worthy of admiration and appreciation.

Dr. Ashok Sachdeva's translation of Dr. Yogendra Nath Shukla's short stories is a testament to his exceptional skills as an English translator. Through his work, he brings to life the microcosms of Indian society depicted in the stories, allowing readers to explore the profound themes, incisive satire, and deep characterizations. His invaluable contribution in making these remarkable stories accessible to a wider audience, transcending language barriers and fostering a deeper appreciation for Indian literature. Some of the following features are worth mentioning during the process of translation:

1. Impeccable Language Proficiency: The translation work exhibits an exceptional command of both Hindi and English. His mastery of language allows him to capture the essence of Dr. Shukla's stories with precision and eloquence. The translated text flows seamlessly, retaining the original style and literary beauty, while ensuring readability for English-speaking audiences.

2. Sensitivity to Cultural Nuances: Effective translation involves more than just converting words from one language to another; it requires an understanding of the cultural nuances embedded in the original work. His translations reflect his deep

---

RESIDENCE : F-43, Shastri Nagar, Meerut - 250 004 (U.P.)
Mob. : 9410454723 • E-mail : drvikas.27nov@gmail.com, vikassharmaccsu@gmail.com

## CH. CHARAN SINGH UNIVERSITY, MEERUT
### DEPARTMENT OF ENGLISH

Dr. VIKAS SHARMA
D.Lit
Professor & Head

General Secretary
The Association for
English Studies of India
(AESI)

Ref No............................................................................................Dated........................

appreciation for the cultural context and societal intricacies portrayed by Dr. Shukla. He adeptly conveys the cultural idiosyncrasies, customs, and values, enabling readers to fully immerse themselves in the stories.

3. Attention to Emotional Resonance: Dr. Shukla's stories often evoke deep emotions, ranging from joy and compassion to sorrow and introspection. Dr. Sachdeva's translation preserves the emotional resonance of the original text, allowing readers to experience the same emotional impact as the original audience. Through his careful selection of words and phrasing, he ensures that the readers connect with the characters and their experiences on a profound level.

4. Maintaining Narrative Flow: Translating short stories requires maintaining a cohesive narrative flow while condensing the essence of the original work. Dr. Sachdeva skillfully navigates this challenge, ensuring that the translated stories maintain their structural integrity and pacing. His ability to capture the essence of each story in a concise format showcases his storytelling acumen and expertise as a translator.

5. Commitment to Accessibility: Dr. Sachdeva's translation work plays a crucial role in promoting cultural exchange and accessibility to literature. By translating, he opens the doors for readers who may not be proficient in Hindi to engage with these captivating narratives. His dedication to making literature accessible to a wider audience reflects his belief in the power of storytelling to transcend linguistic barriers.

6. Collaboration with the Author: A successful translation often requires collaboration and communication with the original author. His collaboration with Dr. Shukla demonstrates his commitment to capturing the author's intent and vision accurately. Through their partnership, they have ensured that the translated stories retain the authenticity and creative essence envisioned by the author, further enhancing the readers' experience.

RESIDENCE : F-43, Shastri Nagar, Meerut - 250 004 (U.P.)
Mob. : 9410454723 • E-mail : drvikas.27nov@gmail.com, vikassharmaccsu@gmail.com

## CH. CHARAN SINGH UNIVERSITY, MEERUT
### DEPARTMENT OF ENGLISH

**Dr. VIKAS SHARMA**
D.Lit
Professor & Head

**General Secretary**
The Association for
English Studies of India
(AESI)

Ref No............................                                    Dated............................

these captivating narratives. His dedication to making literature accessible to a wider audience reflects his belief in the power of storytelling to transcend linguistic barriers.

6. Collaboration with the Author: A successful translation often requires collaboration and communication with the original author. His collaboration with Dr. Shukla demonstrates his commitment to capturing the author's intent and vision accurately. Through their partnership, they have ensured that the translated stories retain the authenticity and creative essence envisioned by the author, further enhancing the readers' experience.

Dr. Ashok Sachdeva's translation of Dr. Yogendra Nath Shukla's short stories is truly commendable. Through his exceptional skills, he has brought these micro-stories to life in English, ensuring that their illuminating, thought-provoking, and intelligent qualities are preserved. His translation enables readers to delve into the depths of Indian society, appreciate the incisive satire, and experience the impact of the characters' realizations.

His translation skills encompass linguistic expertise and a profound understanding of cultural nuances and emotional depth. His translations of Dr. Shukla's short stories captivate readers with their impeccable language proficiency, cultural sensitivity, and ability to convey the intended emotional impact. Dr. Sachdeva bridges language barriers, fosters cultural appreciation, and enables a wider audience to engage with the literary brilliance of Dr. Shukla's stories.

(Prof. Vikas Sharma)

RESIDENCE : F-43, Shastri Nagar, Meerut - 250 004 (U.P.)
Mob. : 9410454313 ▪ E-mail : drvikas.27nov@gmail.com, vikassharmaccsu@gmail.com

www.ingramcontent.com/pod-product-compliance
Lightning Source LLC
LaVergne TN
LVHW041535070526
838199LV00046B/1686